DELVING OF INDIAN WOMENHOOD IN ANITA DESAI 'S NOVEL.

MRS. V. MADHUMIDHA
DR. P. HARSHINI

This book is dedicated to women.

They are strong in their thought, physically and mentally.

Women are the milestones of society.

They are unprecitable as nature.

Contents

Acknowledgements

I wish to thank divine grace of Almighty God, who gave this wonderful chance to write this book.

I sincerely express my deep sense of gratitude to my lovable husband **Er. J. ANBU** for constant moral support and mellifluous affection which helped me to achieve success in every sphere of life and without his kind devotion this book would have been a sheer dream.

I owe and respectfully offer my thanks to my parents for their constructive discussion, perseverance and encouragement during the book writing.

A profound sense of gratitude binds me to my guide and path finder **Dr. P. Harshini** Research Supervisor, Assistant professor, PG & Research Department of English, Ethiraj College for Women, Chennai-08, for her extraordinary cooperation, invaluable guidance and supervision. This book is the result of her painstaking and generous attitude.

I would also extend my special thanks to the institution DR. M. G. R. Educational and Research Institute, Chairperson and Research Department, and superior thanks to the English department.

I am also thankful to my family, friends especially to **T. C. Jayaneela Sneha** who always motivated to do things and for her valuable suggestion and useful comments throughout this book make my dream comes true. And also her way of humor and light- heartedness during this time consuming effort of mine.

I would like to take this opportunity to thank all the persons who have helped in the completion of this book. I also want to thank every single person who ever says, "You have to read this book!" to a friend. I just want people to remind each other how wonderful books are. Readers are the pillars for authors so you are the great treasure for the writer's life. Warm and great thanks to my readers for the valuable comments.

About The Author

Thank you for giving me this wonderful opportunity to introduce myself. V. Madhumidha pursuing her Ph.D. in Dr.M.G.R.Educational and Research Institute, Maduravoyal, Chennai-95. she is native of Perambalur.

She Completed her Bacher Degree at ShrimathiIndraGadhi college Trichy,in the year 2016. She completed her Master's at Bharathidhasan University, Trichy, in 2019. She has presented more than 8 paper in UGC Care Journals. She also two paper in Scopus Indexed Journal.

She have attened more than 15 FDP and Workshops. She is interested in Indian writing, specially Feminism is her excited topic to disscus.

Dr. Harshini. P completed her UG in English Literature from S.D.N.B. Vaishnav College, Chromepet, Chennai. Following this, she did her professional degree course in Library and Information science (UG & PG) from Madras University. Her love for language and literature kept lingering in her and drove hertowards higher studies in English literature. She completed her Doctorate in the subject in the year 2015 from Presidency College, Chennai. She has been an active person in the research field and has contributed a lot to the development of research mainly through her language skills.

She currently serves as Assistant Professor in the Post Graduate and Research Department of English at Ethiraj College for Women, Chennai and also serves as a freelance Editor and Content Writer. She has won many awards including the Best Teacher Award by Mannavar Ullam, Chennai. She has presented and published nearly 50 papers at the National and International level. She is a content writer for many subjects and takes keen interest when it comes to writing in any form. She has donned many roles such as resource person, member in advisory board of International Conferences, Session chair in national and international conferences, programme host and so on. She has posted nearly 45 videos on the subject (English) in the Dr. MGR University Phase II Digital Learning YouTube channel and has organised many webinars, e-workshops, e-FDPs and Virtual Guest lectures. She is also reviewer for two international journals, one based in Canada and another based in Pakistan. She also holds the position of Managing Editor of Englishers International based in Turkey.

She is also an avid reader and a Mehendi artist. Her two books on Mehendi Designs were published by Book Palace Publication, New Delhi and she has also participated in many Mehendi competitions winning prizes each time. She has been as judge too to various art and craft competitions held in the city to evince her keen interest in arts.

I

INTRODUCTION

Anitha Desai was born in Mussoorie on the 24th June 1937 of mixed parentage a Bengali father and a German mother, she was to be benefited by the diverse influences which led to the fermentation of her poetic imagination. At a tender age of seven, she began to write prose, and published some small pieces in children's magazine. She had her education-first at Queen Mary's school, and then at Miranda House, Delhi University, where she took her Bachelor's degree in English literature in 1957.

Anita Desai has several books to her credit which include *Cry, the Peacock* (1963), *Voices in the City* (1965), *Bye-Bye Blackbird* (1971), *Where shall we go this summer?* (1975), *Fire on the Mountain* (1977), (for which she won Royal Society of Literature's of Letters Award, Clear Light of Day (1980), *The Village by the Sea* (1982) *In Custody* (1984), (which was short listed for the 1984 Booker Prize). *Baumgartner's Bombay* (1988), Fasting, Feasting (1999) and her latest novel *Journey To Ithaca*. Desai's short stories have been collected under the title *Games of Twilight* (1978). Besides these novels, her review articles and interviews are considered to be the epitomes of fictional interest and flavour.

Desai's characters are intense, self absorbed, even morbidly so, possessed by a conscience that never allows them peace of mind, constantly analyzing, probing and questioning, merciless in its passion for introspection.

Anita Desai has added a new dimension to Indo-Anglian fiction by concentrating on the exploration of the troubled psyche of her characters, especially, the women in particular. The women writers in Indo-Anglian fiction have shown greater understanding and strength to dig deep into the psyche of the Indian characters. She has depicted through her characters, feminine personality and feminine psyche better than other Indo-Anglian novelists.

Anita Desai does not easily fit into traditional molds, and the scholarly criticism written in reference to her body of work illustrates this by its variety of themes, topics and opinions.Most scholars agree that Desai uses mundane, everyday activities and the seemingly ordinary domain in order to portray something greater and universal, in an existentialist sense, although identifying and describing exactly what that something greater is is where most of the consensus among critics ends. In the five-volume set Indian Women Novelists (1991) edited by R. K. Dhawan, scholars comment on such diverse elements as the alienated self, childhood, marital disharmony, forgotten men, views of nature, cities and gardens, imagery as a mode of apprehension, comparisons to Virginia Woolf, rhythm, the individual's search for identity, the feminine psyche, artists, heroism and pathos, varieties of loneliness, and the polarities of imagination. Just this one work alone illustrates the variety and extensive amount of criticism Desai's body of work has elicited, a sign that although critics do not always agree, her writing is generating great interest and exploration in more than one area of literary theory.

Critic Claire Messud, for example, highlights Desai's ability to use the familiar realm of the everyday and remarks in a review that Desai is "a mistress of synecdoche, a writer whose delicate portraits of the quotidian resonate outwards to convey tumultuous swathes of history," a view that is commonly evoked in regards to Desai's fiction (Hunter 3). K. D. Verma, in turn, applauds Desai for what he sees as important contributions to the literary canon of postcolonial literature claiming "the poststructuralist and postmodernist correction in which Desai's work participates brings (3). Although Desai's works have been received in mostly positive ways in both India and abroad, some critics feel that her characters are generally unheroic, since they do not claim autonomy and are powerfully swayed by outside historical and social forces. Others declare that Desai's perception of the world as an educated middle-class expatriate makes her experiences, and therefore her writing, relatable only to a specific subset within India and lacks universal themes that could pertain to large populations of people.

Although there are a variety of ways to look at Desai's work, and multiple ways to go about analyzing and exploring her fiction, this paper seeks to examine the variety of ways that the maternal is represented in the writings of Anita Desai and to question what types of policies, politics, and mythologies inform and create the societal role of the Indian mother within AngloIndian fiction. In order to investigate the complex and often inconsistent realm wherein Indian mothers dwell within Indo-Anglian fiction, one must look not only at the daily realities and the multiplicity of experiences Indian mothers have but also the historical and mythical constructions which shape the archetypal and idealistic portrayals to which Indian women are constantly compared. Critic Anita Myles affirms that Desai's literature allows an exploration of these themes:

Desai's novels constitute together the documentation, through fiction, of radical female resistance against a patriarchally defined concept of normality. She finds the links between female duality, myth and psychosis intriguing; each heroine is seen as searching for, finding and absorbing or annihilating the double who represents the socially impermissible aspects of her femininity. (36)

One must have a balanced view of each one of these characteristics that make up the complex reality of Indian motherhood to comprehend what it means to subscribe to the societal role of mother in India. Literary critic Ashok Kumar also adds that in her novels there is "the world of radical female resistance against a defined concept of normality and in her psychological novels; she has created the image of a suffering woman preoccupied with her inner world, her sulking frustration and the storm within – the existential predicament of a woman in a male-dominated society" (26).

Additionally, Desai's novels portray a subjective reality wherein characters are shaped by their own and others' perceptions, and identity is in constant flux. Investigating motherhood within this style of writing requires a more nuanced analysis where one can see the subjective, complex and often conflicting realm of Indian motherhood. Lastly, as scholar Brajush Kumar relates in his essay "Feminist Perspectives in the Novels of Anita Desai," "what is more significant about her technique is that she never tries to justify the actions of the women protagonists in her fictional world but grants freedom to act in their own ways. In this way, she has made a sincere endeavor to contribute to the Indian fiction with a feminist concern, though she has carefully avoided associating herself with any feminist movement" (71-2).

II

Anita Desai's Significance in the Exploration of Indian Motherhood

In his book "Women Writing About Women: Feminist Perspectives in Indian Women's Novel in English," Santosh Gupta describes the history of Indian women's writing in English, which emerged in the nineteenth century after it was introduced "into the antahpuras of some aristocratic liberal Indians" (73). He goes on to state that in the twentieth century, Indian women writing in English explored a women's world "that was beginning to be influenced by the emergence of educated self-conscious women....Woman's relation with the new society generated in the consciousness of the changing milieu which is reflected in the writing of this period," of which most is characterized as belonging to the literary genre of social realism (80- 1). Social realism is defined in the Oxford English Dictionary as "The realistic depiction of contemporary (esp. working-class) life as a means of social or political comment," and this form was used by many Indian novelists during the time of the Independence Movement1 as a means to dispel inaccurate portrayals of India, especially in terms of its colonial past, and also to raise awareness of significant issues such as communalism, dowry murders, and caste violence in the Western world.

Anita Desai does draw on this tradition some, and as Santosh Gupta relates, there is commonality between her novels and the novels of Nayantara Sahgal, who both "portray the acute sense of entrapment and suffering of women in the upper and lower middle classes" (85). Literary critic Dhawan situates Anita Desai as a writer outside of this movement, though, stating that she ushered in a new era of psychological realism in this genre [referring to IndoAnglian fiction] with her novel Cry, the Peacock in 1963. Her novels are materially different from those of other eminent Indian women novelists writing in English, such as Kamala Markandaya, Ruth Prawer Jhabvala and Nayantara Sahgal who concern themselves mainly with social and political themes of the East-West encounter. Anita Desai's serious concern is with 'the journey within' of her characters, the chief protagonists being female characters. (12)

Although Anita Desai emerged as a writer during a time period when female Indian writers were actively exploring this genre of social realism, her fiction clearly belongs in a different realm, the realm of modernism. Despite the ability of social realism to accurately portray lived experiences,

Desai's preoccupation with the inner psychic distress of her main characters and their personal struggles to define and assert an individual identity yields itself more easily to a modernist novel construction. Scholar Brajesh Kumar agrees with this assertion and claims that "among these eminent Indian women novelists writing novels in English, Anita Desai is one, who is more interested in the interior landscape of the mind rather than in politics or socio-political realities" (65). Writing in a prescribed format, she would not be able to explore the mythical aspects of Indian femininity while simultaneously exploring entirely individual responses to specific incidents, thereby increasing the complexity of her female characters and reducing the risk of homogenization and essentialist representations.

Desai has often commented that she was greatly influenced by the works of Virginia Woolf and Russian writers such as Fyodor Dostoevsky, and it is clear after reading her novels that this is unquestionably the case. Her style and investigation of feminine sensibility is reminiscent of that in Woolf's To the Lighthouse, among other works. Asha Kanwar notes the similarities between the two authors in her essay "Anita Desai and Virginia Woolf: A Comparative Study," clearly identifying both authors' preoccupation with the way time, memory, and nostalgia operate over a long time period, changing histories and changing the perceptions of the people involved. Kanwar notes similarities in both novelists' works:

there is a constant shift from past to present to future. The past is defined in terms of human memories and the future in terms of human expectations. There is an underlying strain of longing for the past, of nostalgia....It informs not only the content of their work, but shapes the structure as well. For it posits two different times – the present and a longed-for past, upon which the whole novel can be built....we find almost obsessive involvement with the character's past as a key to their consciousness, their life. A preoccupation with Nostalgia and Memory thus becomes an integral part of their craft. (11, 20)

As is the case in Virginia Woolf's famous work A Room of One's Own, female characters in Desai's novels similarly search for an independent identity and place to call their own, a place safe from patriarchal intervention and male domination. Desai's use of narrative voice and her investigation of the psyches of her female characters allow for further insight into her protagonists and also question what constitutes identity and what identity means for different women. Kanwar's delineation of Woolf's goals as a novelist compare with Desai's and include "the exploration of the human personality so as to attain a vision of life's meaning. Her characters live, think and unfold in time and hence her preoccupation underlies her concern with the phenomena of memory, change and death and drives her to ask several different questions" (15).

In Anita Desai's short article "A Secret Connivance" (1990), she states, "If literature, if art has any purpose then it is to show one, bravely and uncompromisingly, the plain face of truth, and here in the West, just as in the East, we must learn to distinguish and recognize, and to value. Once you have told the truth, you have broken free of society, of its prisons. You have entered the realm of freedom" (976). This point made by Desai in regards to her fiction writing encapsulates her artistic intent in literature: to portray truthfully and realistically complex characters that transcend stereotypes or simplistic images. Although she declares that she is not interested in social and political commentary, her honest characterizations of both men and women allow numerous insights into authentic Indian experiences and opens space for scholarly criticism and debate. Most critics focus upon her depictions of Indian women, using her multidimensional female characters to challenge typical representations of Indian women in literature that commonly either evoke the mythical woman or the eternal oppressed victim.

In contrast, her fiction makes a new space in which Indian women might explore selfhood, and she does not place any limits or constraints on how that identity can be discovered. In order to map the daily realities of Indian women, and to investigate the developments of the autonomous female self as depicted in fiction, a critic must look at novels that show the heterogeneity of Indian women's experiences and explore what those experiences foreground. Anita Desai's novels offer a variety of female characters that span the entire spectrum of Indian femininity, and through the various characters she investigates feminine sensibility and the female psyche. Desai has been a writer for over thirty years, and so her novels also span decades, easily illustrating how Indian gendered self-identity has changed and developed over time in response to a variety of native and foreign factors. It is clear through both Desai's fiction and her comments on the subject that she is interested in breaking down stereotypical representations, whether these be of Indian women, Indian mothers, or India in general, and she challenges her readers to do the same. In "A Secret Connivance," for instance, she states that the West has two fixed notions about India. One is that it is a romantic land, full of holy men, maharajas, palaces and elephants: the other is of India as a land of horrors – a place of intolerable poverty and squalor, hunger and disease. How can one country have two such contradictory images? The reason is that neither is true – each is only a half-truth. You may have been made familiar with the face of the maharaja and the face of the beggar child, but have you learnt anything of the human being within? (976)

This question she asks of readers, and Western readers in particular, is indicative of what she is exploring in her novels, how stereotypical representations inform depictions and perceptions of people and why those stereotypes need to be revealed, explored, and broken down. In order to understand Indian mothers, one needs to note the variety of circumstances and experiences that affect and shape each individual person without resorting to a formulaic illustration imposed onto an entire community, nation, or gender.

Specifically, this paper focuses on Anita Desai's concern with the way mythical and ideological representations of Indian women contort and make the image of motherhood and maternity prescriptive within the context of her novels and, of course, in the larger Indian society. Figures such as Sita and the mother goddess constrain Indian women in two explicit ways, since they imply that every woman should be a mother but at the same time present an ideal which no woman can attain. In "Mapping Motherhood: The Fiction of Anita Desai," literary critic Geetanjali Chanda notes that Desai often "weaves the traditional duality of the mother as creator and destroyer and embeds the text in an Indian reality where actual mothers are often ignored or ill-treated; whereas in folklore, myth and nation building the idea of motherhood is venerated and iconic mothers are worshipped" (75). Critic Radha Chakravarty agrees and adds that "in India, women's self-worth and value are usually dependent on their reproductive functions. This valorization of motherhood has its own built-in paradoxes: maternity is associated with a capacity for voluntary self-sacrifice which entitles the mother to her quasidivine status" (77).

Although there is much about Desai's fiction that lends itself easily to the exploration of the female psyche and the effects the Indian social order has upon Indian mothers, her exploration is not necessarily a complete picture of Indian women. Desai often focuses on middle – to upper-class women, which is clearly not representative of even half of India's population, a fact one should keep in mind while reading her work. Some critics have criticized Desai for this elitism, but as she states in "A Secret Connivance," her purpose is to portray honestly unique characters, and since her background is unmistakably middle – to upper-class, it makes sense that she wishes only to depict the experiences and psychological workings of this specific, familiar class group. Although Anita Desai does portray a limited class, she does not fall into the trap of essentializing Indian women, or mothers in particular, vividly illustrating instead the variety of complexities and intricacies through her female characters and their search for their own authentic sense of Indian motherhood and also their own sense of authentic self.

Another qualifier often made by critics of Anita Desai is that she is writing about India in a novel format explicitly not the social realist novel and, further, in English. If she were writing in the style and for the purposes often ascribed to Nayantara Sahgal or Kamala Markandaya in English, they argue, her work would make more sense since the purpose of the social realist novel has often been to raise the consciousness of the Western world and to represent the actual reality of Indian life, but to write in English about the deep, complicated realms of the psyches of Indian upper–class characters appears to cater to a specific readership in India and, in essence, to negate much of Indian life. Although English fluency is greatly on the rise in India, Desai's novels will be most read by the Indian elite, the educated middle and upper classes. Indian critics also add that on top of the limited readership within India, English itself is too easily associated with India's colonial past. Literary critic Meena Alexander illustrates this fear of colonialism via language choice declaring, "Language has of course been an immensely controversial issue for Indian writers, the colonial trappings of English, when raised to consciousness, impossible to evade" (368).

Despite this viewpoint, Desai's association with and eventual choice of English as her medium for expression seems less of a means to make a political statement and merely the consequence of a series of circumstances. These circumstances include a mixed heritage of Bengali and German, and an extensive education conducted in English. Desai has continually contended that English was simply the first language she was taught and thus became the obvious medium through which she expressed her thoughts in writing. Desai remarks in her essay "The Indian Writer's Problems" that "according to the rules laid down by critics, I ought to be writing half my work in Bengali and the other half in German. As it happens, I have never written a word in either language. Possibly I found English to be a suitable link language, a compromise. But I can state definitely that I did not choose English in a deliberate and conscious act" (7). She further goes on to explain that "By writing novels that have been catalogued by critics as psychological, and that are purely subjective, I have been left free to employ, simply, the language of the interior" (9).

India's struggle with colonialism had numerous effects on almost every aspect of Indian culture, and the social constructions of Indian femininity and motherhood were not exempt. During the independence movement, many different people from a variety of political perspectives were involved in claiming India as an autonomous country, one that should not be ruled by outsiders. The majority of Indians involved in the movement tried to assert not only India's worth and need for independence from colonial rule but also the cultural distinctions which made India different and separate from Great Britain and, inevitably, the Western world. In her book Dislocating Cultures: Identities, Traditions and Third-World Feminism, Uma Narayan discusses how this virile national agenda shaped the dichotomy between the East and West, and also how numerous things were coded as either good or bad based on this dichotomy:

A critical understanding of the 'cultural distinctions' constructed in colonial struggles is salient to contemporary Third-World feminist agendas. Anticolonial struggles for national independence in many Third-World countries not only rejected the legitimacy of Western colonial rule but also often constructed a nationalist political identity by contrasting the indigenous "culture" and "its values" to those of the West, calling for a rejection of the latter. (14)

This rejection of western values was not all encompassing, though, and Narayan explores which things were coded as essentially Western and which things were not, contesting that concepts such as feminism were inevitably seen as Western, while other things, such as technological advances, were seen as progress. She states that Third World feminists are often seen as "incarnations of a colonized consciousness, the views of 'privileged native women in whiteface,' seeking to attack their 'non-Western culture' on the basis of 'Western' values" (3). She then questions the policies of the nationalist movement and attempts to reveal problems and paradoxes within the nationalistic ideologies, while also questioning what motivates them. For Narayan, the rejection of feminism as a Western construct is a way to disempower the indigenous movement and the women involved, characterizing them not as individuals with their own specific political agendas but as imitators, merely mimicking Western ideas of female autonomy and independence. She declares that Third World feminists need to contest not only specific practices and institutions but also challenge "the larger pictures of Nation, History and Cultural Traditions that serve to sustain and justify these practices and institutions" (20-21).

Lastly, it is important to mention how idealizations of an independent India evident in nationalistic narratives that declare India is homogenous and in direct opposition to colonial rule become representative of the idea of India but not the reality of the Indian population as a whole. Narayan argues that depictions of India evoked by nationalists should be categorized as totalizing pictures that cast values and practices that pertained to specific privileged groups within the community as values of the 'culture' as a whole. In the case of anticolonial India nationalism, 'Indian culture' was often problematically equated with aspects of upper-caste Hindu culture, ignoring the actual cultural and religious diversity of the Indian population. (15)

This view of totalizing discourse is also shared by Edward Said, a postcolonial literary theorist who is quoted by Shubha Tiwari as making a distinction between discourses of deformation which he calls "gigantic caricatural essentialisms" and the reformation of open-ended discourse which takes account of all the minute "affinities, sympathies and compassion" (264). Tiwari goes on to say that he believes Desai shares the same perspective as Said since the characterization of people portrayed within her novels rejects "people as representatives" (264). In order to explore the complex societal role of motherhood, it is important to have access to discourses that are not essentializing, homogenous representations of India women. Just like American women or Chinese women, Indian women, especially as represented in Desai's fiction, are complex and dynamic. Sometimes they are oppressed, but other times they are not. Sometimes they are even able to find powerful positions within oppressive institutions or situations, and by consistently making sure that the discourse and rhetoric one uses is fully encompassing the multifaceted experiences of women, one can make a closer examination and gain greater insight.

Historically, even in western literature Indian women are most often depicted as docile, yet explicitly sexual beings decidedly oppressed under the burdens of Indian patriarchy, with little option to have a life different from the generations of subjugated women who lived in the generations prior. One such example of this is Katherine Mayo's *Mother India* (1927), a piece that attacked Hindu society and its customs from her perspective as an outsider and proponent of imperialism. Looking at her work now, eighty years later, it appears racist and essentialist although it is also representative of much of the literature written by the West in regards to the East during that time period. Scholar Joanna Liddle writes in her essay "Feminism, Imperialism and Orientalism: the Challenge of the 'Indian

Woman'" that "the racism of such writing becomes explicit where Mayo contends that Indian habits and attitudes are a danger, not just to themselves but to the rest of the world, and contrasts the culture of the 'Anglo-Saxon', which leads him into 'the full glory of manhood', with that of the Indian, which produces 'broken-nerved, low spirited, petulant ancients'" (503). Even though there are obviously women and men in India who fit into such stereotypes, there are many who do not, and this portrayal leaves little room for their voices and experiences to be heard as anything other than unique and non-normative. Scholar Ania Loomba declares this same point:

many writings on postcolonialism emphasise concepts like 'hybridity' and fragmentation and diversity, and yet they routinely claim to be describing 'the postcolonial condition', or 'the postcolonial subject' or 'the postcolonial woman'. At best such terms are no more than a helpful shorthand, because they do not allow for differences between distinct kinds of colonial situations, or the workings of class, gender, location, race, caste or ideology among people whose lives have been restructured by colonial rule" ("Colonialism" 19).

Further, since many feminists in the western world tend to assume that motherhood is almost always constraining and for some represents a way that women can be controlled and patriarchy maintained, Indian mothers are seen as doubly oppressed.

Anita Desai is not considered explicitly feminist in the way female Indian authors such as Nayantara Sahgal and Ruth Prawar Jhabvala are often characterized, but many critics do assert that the overall messages her novels portray are synonymous with feminist messages. Feminist scholar Elizabeth Jackson, for instance, contends that most of Desai's female protagonists are "middle-class Indian women who are at odds with the cultural norms which shape their lives, and her fiction seeks to unravel their complex responses to the limitations imposed by culturally sanctioned codes of feminine thought and behaviour" (33). Additionally, her exploration of the family and the home, historically female domains, as well as her focus on female characters and the feminine dilemmas of marriage, child-bearing, care-taking and widowhood add insight into how Indian femininity and, more specifically, Indian motherhood is constructed and maintained within society. For Third-World feminists and those seeking to learn more about Indian feminism, her exploration of the complexity of femininity is the most important part of her "critique." Third-World feminism seeks to define itself not in opposition to First-World feminism but as an independent movement, seeking to look at specific doctrines, institutions, and national processes and how these shape women's lives in both positive and negative ways.

Many Western feminists find that motherhood is idealized, and when women actually have children, they are alienated from their reproductive labor, but it is also impossible for them to condemn motherhood completely because despite its hardships, many women ultimately find it satisfying. Like Western feminists, Indian feminists are exploring motherhood and making similar conclusions, conclusions that place motherhood in an arena where one can see both the oppressive constraints and powerful, hopeful responses it elicits. Further, Veena Poonacha during her investigation of motherhood in south India found that sometimes "women's experiences of rearing and nurturing children has created a unique culture, which provides a counterpoint to critique masculinist norms of dominance" (101).

III

Discussion of Fire on the Mountain, Clear Light of Day, and Fasting, Feasting

In order to look at different configurations of the maternal, and to investigate how Indian mothers assume power within different, seemingly oppressive contexts, this paper is going to focus on three novels by Anita Desai: Fire on the Mountain (1977), Clear Light of Day (1980), and Fasting, Feasting (1999). Although Desai examines the complexities of the female psyche and the search for self-identity in many of her novels, these three novels span decades and generations, allowing for a detailed investigation of what it means to be an Indian mother and how this determines, constrains, and enables the making of the female self. Radha Chakravarty argues that in Desai's novels, the maternal "becomes the site for the articulation of the female desire to determine one's own identity, in confrontation with traditional inscriptions of the mother's body as a means of controlling female subjectivity" (77). The three novels also offer a plethora of female characters to observe, characters that vary in age, class, location, time period, occupation, marital status, child-bearing desire, and sexual practice, among other noticeable descriptions, which differences allow the reader to address not just the role of the Indian mother but also the roles available to those who are non-mothers, whether by choice or fate.

Through these multiple characters, Desai makes sure to stay true to her idea of honest realism, allowing the reader to see multiple configurations of femininity and also the different, often conflicting ways Indian women choose to interact within their gendered, subjective worlds. Critic Meena Shirwadkar, in her book Image of Woman in the Indo-Anglian Novel, argues that "the ideal of womanhood in India is motherhood – that marvelous, unselfish, all suffering, ever-forgiving mother. The wife walks behind, the shadow. So, in the Indian tradition, the wife led a silent, shadowy existence till she became the mother of a son" (79). In the three novels, there are multiple roles that relate to the construction of Indian motherhood that help one to define and explore what it means to be a mother, or not be a mother, in each specific context. That is, within the novels' representations of Indian women, there are good mothers and bad mothers, dutiful mothers and neglectful mothers, widows and virgins, mother-in-laws and daughters, professionals and housewives, aunts and sisters, all of whom characterize and seek to discover not only what it is to be an Indian mother but also what it means when one does not accede to the cultural constructions deemed normative and affirmed as correct behavior within each circumstance. Sangeeta Dutta argues that in Desai's novels as well as in a number of Indo- Anglican novels a dialectical strain can be discerned in literature demonstrating on the one hand the hegemonical gender ideology absorbed by women and on the other subversive female search for selfhood and space....Repetitive fictional techniques, of the symbolic journey and myth reversal, also indicate the shifting authorial concern from the mother confined to the mother in search of self. (93)

The three novels Fire on the Mountain, Clear Light of Day, and Fasting, Feasting fit this model given by Dutta since through these novels Desai exposes the gender ideologies that oppress women and mothers specifically but also shows how those same women are not merely victims but actively searching for ways to create an autonomous self even within the seemingly oppressive confines of the family and the overarching model of Indian motherhood. Critic Chakravarty agrees with this assessment, adding that "the figure of the mother emerges in her novels as a sign of multiple possibilities...with both repressive and emancipatory potential" (75).

Additionally, these novels give further insight into specific gender oppressions afflicting Indian motherhood, focusing upon what Anita Desai terms "one form of imprisonment," the deification and mythical representation of femaleness ("Secret Connivance" 972). The mythicization of Indian motherhood is a cultural construct that defines the way Indian women are perceived, portrayed, and ultimately judged. There are a number of central mythical ideals that uphold a specific, universalizing Indian motherhood: the most prominent in the fiction of Anita Desai include the characterizations of actual Hindu and Vedic goddesses, the cow as a mythical feminine force, and the nationalistic myth of Mother India. These narratives cannot be completely characterized as evil forces strictly aimed against women, and it is important to note that it is not the fact that there are idealistic representations of the Indian mother that is crucial but the fact that these can be used politically to undermine or support a specific oppressive doctrine defining certain essential characteristics that all Indian mothers share. Chakravarty notes that these narratives of mythical women or maternal representations "sought to construct a homogenized, abstract figure of 'woman,' to serve the needs of their respective political agendas, [their denoting anyone using womanhood for implicit political purposes] without any real concern for the divergent needs of actual women in different sectors of Indian society" (76).

In the article "Mapping Motherhood: The Fiction of Anita Desai," scholar Geetanjali Singh Chanda asserts that "the mother figure has been central to Indian arts and ritual practices from as far back as 20,000 BC. The mother goddess was and is worshipped for her awesome powers of creation and protection as well as for her fearsome power of destruction" (73). The mother goddess as an archetypical representation of seemingly ideal Indian motherhood creates a binary whereby supposedly every woman can be placed in either one category or the other. Chanda highlights this binary and describes it as a dual characterization that forces women into the role of good woman or bad woman, with little room for mobility. Women culturally understood as good are wives and mothers who fulfill societal obligations of creation and procreation while women marked as bad are most likely disrupting social expectations, withdrawing from the role of procreation, and causing destruction to their community. Critic Sanjeeta Dutta agrees with this analysis:

> "*In India, a long history of mother-goddess worship legitimizes woman's glorification/deification as the divine mother, the source of energy, power and fertility while the same motherhood is an institutionalized form of oppression and subjugation of women. In a patriarchal kinship structure, a woman's status in the household is determined by her ability to produce male issue for her husband's lineage. Her identity revolves around the wife/mother roles beyond which no individuality needs to be established or recognized. (84)*"

The mother goddess, Sita, Laksmi, Draupadi, and Parvati are just a few of the manifestations of acceptable and glorified femininity that idealize motherhood and wifehood, creating a standard that appears almost impossible for any Indian woman to attain, even the middle – to upper-class women that Desai focuses on in her novels.

Anita Desai herself declares that the idealized Indian female, particularly in the form of Sita, "is meek, docile, trusting, faithful and forgiving. Even when spirited and brave, she adheres to the archetype: willing to go through fire and water, dishonour and disgrace for his [referring to Rama, her husband in the Ramayana epic] sake" ("Secret Connivance" 972). Although Desai is condemning limitations implicit in the figure of Sita, she is not necessarily reproving motherhood or the idea of being a dutiful wife; she merely seeks to illuminate how confining the ideological demands of a mythical motherhood can be and how unacceptable it is within Indian society to try to transgress that model as an Indian woman. Desai affirms that mythological representations of womanhood keep a woman "bemused, bound hand and foot. To rebel against it – either in speech or action – would mean that she is questioning the myth, attacking the legend, and that cannot be permitted: it is the cornerstone on which the Indian family and therefore Indian society are built" (972). Therefore, this Indian myth of true womanhood not only constrains women to a specific role and space within society but also creates a control mechanism of consequences which forces women into culturally appropriate behavior.

The holy cow, a common symbol of India, is another representation that emerges in Desai's fiction as a feminine force and model by which motherhood is characterized. Meena Shirwadkar discusses this phenomenon and documents its complexities:

> "Raja Rao envisions the Matri Shakti or mother-principal as the supreme quality in woman and he sees her at the centre of the family. The mother-image is seen in woman, in animals, in nature, in goddesses. The ancient Vedic image of Gomata cow-mother, is applied to the mother in the family, fusing the universal and the particular. The cow-image is applied to the mother in the family and to mother India...The cow is the symbol of compassion, devotion, protection and bounty, all crystallised in the idea of motherhood. (85-86)"

The cow is a symbol in India, and in the rest of the world, of India's religious devotion and compassion for all sentient beings. It requires assistance to live but also provides protection and sustenance for the owner, producing characteristics that can be readily applied to motherhood. Although the cow is not a commonly evoked image of femininity and motherhood in India, Desai uses it extensively, especially in Clear Light of Day, as a way to show how motherhood is mythicized in India.

The ever-changing pantheon of goddesses present from the Vedic period to modern times in India and the Vedic cow image have been an important part of Indian culture for centuries, but they are not the only aspect of the overall mythicization of the Indian mother. Shirwadkar argues that the mother cow image of the Vedic times eventually morphs into "Mother India during the Ghandian struggle, expanding the sphere of the family with the idea of the universal mother" (86). Many scholars discuss the implications of this model of Mother India. This ideal came to prominence during India's struggle for independence whereby the actual country was likened to one's mother, who obviously needed to be saved from the perverse clutches of imperialistic Great Britain.

Although the tactic of using motherhood in the Indian independence movement proved to be somewhat successful in uniting the country, it also made a claim that there is an authentic, specific experience that can be attributed both to Mother India as a geographic site of a colonial power struggle and to Indian mothers, upon whom this ideal is supposedly based. This form of idealization became very problematic for Indian women who found that, like the Goddess archetype, Mother India was constrained and bound by certain characteristics deemed natural and normal for the Indian mother. Mother India is timeless, the preserver of the ancient cultural traditions of India, in need of protection, ever-sacrificing for her Indian children, and also a land that is caught in between the power struggles of men (both colonial imperialists and Indian men involved in the independence movement).

Meena Alexander's article "Outcaste Power: Ritual Displacement and Virile Maternity in Indian Women Writers" explores this concept of Mother India and adds that the image "was part of the myth making essential to decolonisation. Mother India was tender, nurturing, but also explosive and virile in a manner that has no visible analogue in the western humanist tradition" (370). Alexander even comments on the Gandhian revolution for independence, which strove to end aggressive colonization with the somewhat feminine form of non-violence and also mobilized huge numbers of women into the movement. These women, although seen by Gandhi as actual individual human beings capable of political action, were also glorified for the "moral superiority of female suffering rather than women's ability for political intervention. Instead of playing on the aggressive courage of a warrior queen like the Rani or Jhansi, Gandhi chose to stress the love and internalised suffering of a Sita or Draupadi" (370). He did contend that being a Sita figure was not meant to characterize women as passive or helpless, arguing instead that women found their power in their moral virtue, citing that in the Ramayana, even Ravana could not touch Sita due to her moral superiority.

Although some aspects of the cultural construction of Mother India can easily be regarded as positive attributes, the association of Indian mothers with a geographic piece of land and one that is in constant need of protection and defense is very problematic. Additionally, leaving the burden of cultural transmission and preservation to women, and, specifically, mothers, constrains women not only to transmit Indian societal values to the future generations but also to be the most visible upholders of those same cultural values. For Indian mothers, not to uphold what are deemed the most important values would be the same as saying that one disagrees with the national movement for independence and thus be in league with the colonizers.

Fire on the Mountain

Fire on the Mountain is a novel centered on the character Nanda Kaul, a great-grandmother who has grown disillusioned about her roles as a wife and mother and who, once widowed, moves to Kausali to live a solitary existence free of the confinements of her previous life. The narrator declares that she "had suffered through the nimiety, the disorder, the fluctuating and unpredictable excess. She had been so glad when it was over. She had been glad to leave it all behind, in the plains, like a great, heavy, difficult book that she had read through and was not required to read again" (32). Nanda's reclusive existence is suddenly interrupted with the appearance of Raka, her great-granddaughter, who has been sent to Kausali because her mother is ill and unable to take care of her. The novel follows the psychological struggles of Nanda Kaul as she tries to understand her great-granddaughter Raka and herself. Fire on the Mountain was published in 1977, at the very end of the Indian Emergency Period 2, initiated by Prime Minister Indira Gandhi as a means to settle the political and economic unrest in India. Indira Gandhi and her political party were defeated in the elections of 1977, and the Janata party took over to try to quell the unrest and instability of the period. Indian literature of this period was becoming more open to various topics and complex literary styles, although many female Indian authors in the Indo-Anglican genre, including Ruth Prawar Jhabvala and Rama Mehta, were still focused on the social realist novel.

Literary critic Rama Kundu also asserts that during this time period "the women writers of the last three decades have been giving voice to their aspirations and ordeals as well as the anguish and frustration of the previous generations – their mothers and grandmothers. One of the many ways of expressing this consciousness is voicing the longing for a space of 'her' own, or the anguish at failing to find one" (149). This paper will focus on four female characters in the novel, Nanda Kaul, Raka, her mother Tara, and Nanda Kaul's longtime friend Ila Das. Through those characters, I will explore the mythicization of Indian motherhood through the construction of personas that resemble Hindu goddesses like Sita and Draupadi, what happens when mythical motherhood fails women, and how non-mothers exist in a society where motherhood is central.

In Fire on the Mountain, Nanda Kaul has come to Kausali in order to retire from the world of caring and compassion that she provided without gratitude for so many years. In "The Ideology of Space in Fire on the Mountain," critic Kundu posits that "Kausali is a real empirical space and at the same time it is apparently emblematic of Nanda's protest and assertion, the penultimate act of assertion that she has made at the fag-end of her life, regarding her need of a 'room of one's own'. It seems to be a contrast to the male spaces she has lived in in the past, which were occupied and controlled by her father or husband" (150). In her new life at Kausali, she hopes to forget about all the memories associated with her past as nurturer and to live anisolated life with no one around to bother her. She is disappointed to hear of Raka's arrival and the subsequent interruption of her solitary existence: "It was against the old lady's policy to question her [Asha, her daughter] but it annoyed her that she should once again be drawn into a position where it was necessary for her to take an interest in another's activities and be responsible for their effect and outcome. When would she be done?" ("Fire on the Mountain" 50- 1).

The narrator also states that "the care of others was a habit Nanda Kaul had mislaid. It had been a religious calling she had believed in till she found it fake. It had been a vocation that one day went dull and drought-struck as though its life-spring had dried up" (33). For years, Nanda Kaul bought into the characterization of the Indian mother associated with the so-called 'good' characterizations of mythical Hindu goddesses, particularly Sita or Draupadi, but that course did not bring her any of the fulfillment that she imagined it would and, in fact, led her eventually to renounce that life and remove herself from any nurturing activities or behavior. Ramesh Gupta comments on this choice of hers and remarks, "She prefers seclusion not because she favors it but to rest her pain-filled psyche, her stagnated pulses, bits and pieces of identity that she attempts to get in the shelter of Carignano [her house in Kausali]" (109). Although the reasons behind Nanda's decision to move to Carignano are clear, Desai follows Nanda's new existence and questions if her total removal from the world of motherhood and compassionate, caring behavior actually solves her problem of a trauma-ridden psyche. It is easy to understand why Nanda would decide to go to Carignano and how her life has failed her expectations and has ultimately proved to be unfulfilling for her, but Desai goes further and instead of presenting all the reasons Nanda should renounce, she questions what happens after she does and also inquires if this new existence, free from obligation, is actually fulfilling for her.

Towards the middle of the novel, Nanda begins to develop a fascination with Raka and begins to question if this is the one child with whom she could actually identify herself. She declares, "Raka, you really are a great-grandchild of mine, aren't you? You are more like me than any of my children or grandchildren. You are exactly like me, Raka" (71). Although she sees the connection between herself and Raka, and notices that Raka needs to be nurtured and loved by her, she does not fulfill the obligation. For her it seems that removing one's self from any caretaking situation was easier than actually having a child around and refusing to care for it, and she laments her inability to help. She tries telling Raka elaborate fairy tales in order to make her happy, but then realizes the irony since she herself was told fairy tales and in the end found them to be empty and fake. Indeed, the narrator declares that Nanda bitterly cursed her failure to comfort children, her inability to place herself in another's position and act accordingly. Fantasy and fairy tales had their place in life, she knew it so well. Why then did she not tell the child the truth? Who wanted truth? Who could stand it? Nobody. Not even herself. So how could Raka? (97)

At the end of the novel, Nanda realizes the solace and peace she sought at Carignano was actually as false as the fairy tales she tells Raka about her past. The only reason Nanda is even able to live a comfortable life in her new dwelling is because she has erased her past instead of coming to terms with it. She remembers Miss David, the woman whom her husband truly loved instead of her and how their affair affected her life with her husband. She also remembers her real past, not the one she has woven to tell Raka nor the one she imagines for herself. Scholar Shata Acharya contends that this "tumbling out of her past, this crumbling of her defenses, this final confession, this inexorable humiliation is then what one is left with. This final confrontation with the truth of her situation renders her heroic. The peace that she thought she has finally attained was on fire" (61). Scholar Elizabeth Jackson states that most of the critical literature "interprets this tragic ending as a demonstration of Desai's view that 'one cannot with impunity reject the duties that real life thrusts upon one, no matter how onerous the burden'" (126). So in the end although Nanda sought to escape her existence as a wife and mother, she did not find fulfillment completely rejecting all caring or nurturing behavior or when she left Raka alone, in dire need of love and mothering.

Since Nanda is the main focus of the novel, most of the other women are secondary characters, although Raka and her mother Tara emerge as important figures in the discussion of Indian motherhood. Tara is a woman who, like her grandmother, bought into the ideological construct of Indian motherhood and assumed a subservient role to her husband. Tara is not only unfulfilled by her nurturing roles as a wife and mother but is, further, abused by her husband. Although Asha does not comment on the situation at Raka's home when she asks Nanda to take her in, it is obvious that it is causing trauma in the lives of both Raka and Tara. Literary scholars Premila Paul and R. Padmanabhan Nair write that "Life for a woman is a series of obligations and commitments. Tara gets ill-treated by her husband, but the woman has to yield always. Woman often becomes woman's enemy. Asha attributed Tara's domestic misfortune to her inability to understand men and also her inability to be a successful diplomat's wife," which only reiterates the treatment women such as Tara sometimes receive from other women, but also what expectations Indian society puts on women in abusive situations (231).

Like Sita, Tara is expected to handle whatever comes her way with quiet submissiveness, even if it means abuse to both herself and her child. Nanda Kaul also obviously knows what is really going on since she wonders what will happen to Tara after she is deceased and even thinks of leaving Kausali to her: "perhaps she [Nanda] should leave the house to Tara who needed shelter, a cave to crawl into and die" ("Fire" 113). Raka is just another casualty of Tara's traumatic relationship with Raka's father, and it is obvious through her reclusive behavior and refusal to get close to any human being that she has been profoundly damaged by her home environment. In the novel, she reflects on what she remembers about home and thinks of her father, home from a party, stumbling and crashing through the curtains of night, his mouth opening to let out a flood of rotten stench, beating at her mother with hammers and fists of abuse – harsh, filthy abuse that made Raka cower under her bedclothes and wet the mattress in fright, feeling the stream of urine warm and weakening between her legs like a stream of blood, and her mother lay down on the floor and shut her eyes and wept. Under her feet, in the dark, Raka felt that flat, wet jelly of her mother's being squelching and quivering, so that she didn't know where to put her feet and wept as she tried to get free of it. (79)

It is obvious that Raka needs help and that her early home life has damaged her and her ability to have a successful relationship. Nanda is able to see all of this but refuses to get involved in what she feels will be just another exploitive relationship. In return, Raka roams the desolate landscape trying to find escape, ultimately setting fire to the entire forest around her at the close of the novel, screaming for the attention she has been so deprived of her entire life. R.S. Sharma states that the end of the novel is "expressive of Raka's resolve to destroy a world where a woman cannot hope to be happy without being unnatural," therefore aligning Raka's act of violent destruction with the resistance she feels towards the feminine roles she is already expected to uphold (Gupta 106). Obviously after witnessing so much hurt and unfulfillment within her mother's life, Raka feels like she should run away and try her best not to get caught and forced to submit to being a mother and a wife. Nanda has the opportunity to become basically the only caring person in Raka's life, but, instead, Raka is left to fend for herself and to know only of isolation and loneliness and not the feeling of love or of being a part of a family.

Ila Das, a social worker and old acquaintance of Nanda, emerges as a tragic mother figure and also is the only non-biological mother character one meets in the plot of the novel. She is not a mother and did not ever even get the chance to get married and have children. Although her family was fairly wealthy, her brothers squandered away their inheritance and forced the two adult sisters to begin working in order to squeak out a meager existence. Desai describes the loss of "the family fortune, divided amongst three drunken, dissolute sons as in a story, and not a penny of it to either of the two cleaver, thrifty, hard-working daughters, Ila and Rima" (135). For Ila, Nanda Kaul was always there "standing at a height, like a beacon, like an ideal," and for Ila this ideal was unattainable in her life due to her inability to secure a husband or financial stability (123). When Ila was first forced to enter the working world, she was already then close to the official age for retirement and no matter how low she pitched her demands, there were always bright, carefree young girls to be employed for even less. As for qualifications, Ila Das's were of the gentile sort that are not put on paper and rubber-stamped, and she was turned away by the employment bureau and any employer that she nerved herself to face. (137)

Because her education and upbringing left her completely unprepared for working or living such an impoverished existence, Ila Das can barely get by on the small salary she makes and is constantly hungry and undernourished. Her situation appears to also be a commentary on how education operates for women such as Ila Das and also how colonialism historically shaped middle class education and actually created helpless, dependent girls instead of educated, independent women. Ila Das definitely realizes this and proclaims to Nanda "how helpless our upbringing made us, Nanda. We thought we were being equipped with the very best....my, all that only to find it left us helpless, positively handicapped," and she later argues that a rural upbringing, with the ability to live in a village and rely on natural resources, would have been more beneficial for her actual survival. She does find happiness in her occupation as a social worker, a nurturing occupation that could position her as a mother figure, though Desai does not allow this to be something fundamentally empowering for Ila. Instead of becoming her means of autonomy and independence, and a way for her to fulfill her desire to nurture, her job as a social worker becomes a threat and ends up being the ultimate downfall for her. After trying to stop a child marriage which was arranged only for monetary gain, she is confronted by the father of the child bride who seeks to end her meddling. He ends up raping and killing her in order to prove his point that men rule women, and afterwards the narrator describes Ila "Crushed back, crushed down into the earth, she lay raped, broken, steel and finished. Now it was dark" (156).

Ila is powerless in the face of the father, like so many other mothers and mother figures. Ila's long turbulent life comes to an end there, her lying face down in the dirt, exposed and defiled. Ila Das' one foray into an acceptable form of nurturing behavior and a validation of the characteristics of Indian motherhood ultimately ends in her violent rape and death, perhaps a commentary on the life to be led by single, poor women, raised middle class but without the means for individual survival within Indian society. Literary critic Elizabeth Jackson also contends that "In India it can be argued that the threat of sexual violence does keep women in their place, literally as well as figuratively, and a number of writers have noted the resulting restrictions on women's mobility" (53). Also, Geetha Ramanthan "has suggested that the sexual violence here [In Ila's case] has its own terrible logic as a punishment for a woman who interferes with men's transactions of female sexuality" (71). Overall, Ila's unfortunate circumstances can be viewed as a commentary of the lives available to single, poor women in India but also the sexual violence that results in any context of patriarchal domination.

Clear Light of Day

Clear Light of Day is a novel that examines the interactions of two middle-aged sisters, Bimla ("Bim") and Tara Das, during a visit by Tara to their ancestral home in Old Delhi where Bim still resides. The story jumps back and forth between the present day (1980) and the sisters' childhood memories of Delhi during the traumatic partition and independence of India. Throughout the novel, Desai reveals more and more details about Bim and Tara's childhood which eventually shape how the reader characterizes the adult versions of the sisters and their actions. This time period in Indo-Anglian literature is similar to what was stated earlier in regards to Fire on the Mountain, with female Indian writers exploring more complex themes and pursuing ideas surrounding the concepts of identity and purpose. In 1980, the actual country of India was again under the leadership of Indira Gandhi, although sectarian violence and unrest still remained. The characters Bim, Tara, Mira-masi, Mother and the Misra sisters all add complexity to the discussion of Indian motherhood and also demonstrate how maternity and matrimony shape Indian women's lives. Chakravarty does note, however, that at the end of the novel, the figure of the mother still emerges as a complicated enigma, "a sign of multiple possibilities, a trope with both repressive and emancipatory potential" (75). In this novel, Desai also explores how female identity is formed and how self-reflection and memory operate in the female psyche. Within the story, motherhood can be characterized in a variety of ways, including through the nationalistic myth of mother India, the cow as a mythical feminine force, and the appropriation of characteristics of particular goddesses. It is also interesting to see how women who are not mothers are characterized within the social order of the novel and to investigate exactly what it means either to have access to or to be denied access to the societal role of mother.

Throughout the story, Bim Das is the person who holds the entire Das family together. She has to nurse her brother Raja back to health, take care of her other mentally-challenged brother, Baba, and keep an eye on her self-destructive, alcoholic Mira-masi all while trying to assert an independent self and oversee the affairs necessary to keep the house in order. At one point Bim laments, "I wish there was someone else who would go [on an errand]....there is never anybody except me" (61). From a very young age, Bim is under the burden of a number of responsibilities, and there is a constant tension between what the family requires of her for its survival and what Bim wants for herself. At one point in the novel Bim proclaims, "I don't understand the insurance business. Father never bothered to teach me. For all father cared, I would have grown up illiterate and – and cooked for my living, or swept. So I had to teach myself history, and teach myself to teach," illustrating exactly how she feels about her bringing and the lack of preparation it gave her for her actual future responsibilities (155).

It is not only Bim's father that makes her feel she is unprepared, but later in her life her brother Raja also does not understand the encumbrances Bim has. Leaving her to care for the insurance business and renouncing any duties he would have had as the eldest son, Raja ignores how vulnerable she is economically as a single woman, "binding her to the very familial system she has wanted to escape. Bim's attempts to deal with her femininity as a controllable obstacle that can be overcome through education and willpower have not changed the fundamental distribution of social and economic power which ultimately demands that she pay the price for her brother's freedom" (Valjento 188). Like the house in Old Delhi, she remains static even when everything around her is changing. In a way the house itself can be seen as representative of India during the time of the partition and beyond, while Bim, its keeper, is emblematic of Mother India, the caretaker of the nation.

Like the mythical construct Mother India, Bim is not an actual biological mother, although in both cases that fact is not important; what is significant is that both Bim and Mother India have the characteristics deemed integral to motherhood and therefore can draw on the power of the myth to assert their individual persona, and in Bim's case to gain autonomy and mobility in her own right. Literary critic Sangeeta Dutta investigates this phenomenon, noting that "Desai raises the question whether rejecting physical motherhood is really rebellious. Bim has chosen to remain single, and seems antithetical to her sister Tara whose sole concentration is on her family and children. But though Bim had not physically been a life giver – her nurturing abilities are emphasized" (92). Dutta goes on to say that "Bim achieves the identity of archetypal sustainer....by commitment to uphold relationships. Bim's symbolic motherhood sustains the family and also the house becomes a life giving and sustaining force against the destructive outer world" (92). So again, the important part for the characterization and representation of the maternal is not physical, biological motherhood but, rather, the nurturing and caring role within each individual family unit, the role that Bim occupies within the Das household.

At first, Bim's burdens way heavily on the reader and make one feel mostly pity for her character and the life that she is forced to lead. In a telling anecdote, Tara remembers the time that Bim was attacked by a swarm of bees, and the narrator proclaims "It was a bees' festival, a celebration, Bim their appointed victim, the sacrificial victim on whom they had draped the ceremonial shawl, drawing it close about her neck as she stood drooping, shivering under the weight of their gauzy wings, their blue-black humming" (135). Although this story is merely that of a childhood incident, it represents both the weight of responsibility that fell onto Bim's shoulders after the death of her parents and a marker of the guilt that her sister Tara felt at abandoning her family in order to pursue the more leisurely life of being Bakul's wife and the mother to his children. Bim, like Mother India, is merely the necessary victim, someone chosen to epitomize the traditions and rituals that symbolize India, even if that means complete self sacrifice.

The nation should always be prioritized as more important than the individual, and it is fitting that Bim, an individual, is attacked by a hive of bees, all acting in tandem and with the same interests. After Bim is attacked by the bees and forced to submit, she takes on the weight of the societal burdens and is actually brought close to resignation because of the immense encumbrance of responsibilities. Scholar Jenni Valjento actually feels that the entire novel rests on Bim's conflicted identity, her want to transcend the traditional role normally ascribed to Indian women but also her need to take care of the family and her family members. She states that Bim's identity formation consists of "a series of efforts to break free of an unwanted seclusion: isolated between the pathologically unchanging home and the prospect of adopting an equally restrictive upper middle-class female identity, Bim strives to be included in the changing outside world" (187).

Despite the heavy burdens Bim is forced to endure alone, without the help of her able siblings Tara and Raja, she still emerges as a positively characterized model and one who is not easily defined and placed within societal structures. Literary critic Valjento claims that "Bim's cynicism [later in her life] comes from having no opportunities to act and be perceived as the kind of woman she originally wanted to be, and from a repeated obligation to be the woman others need to see her as," but I think most people look back on their lives and the desires they had when they were young and feel that they did not live up to their original expectations. Although Bim has obviously had to conform to certain roles within the family and as a woman, at the end of the novel Bim appears to reconcile these feelings and realize how her family and home life truly shaped both her and Tara's perceptions. Although she was forced to become the caretaker for her family and put her life plans on hold, Bim is able to use this to her advantage, refusing to marry and later becoming a teacher who has the ability to earn money outside of the home. She declares, "'I shall work – I shall do things'….'I shall earn my own living – and look after Mira-masi and Baba and – and be independent'" (140). Through her unique yet restrictive upbringing, she sees the potential for liberation and the ability to assert one's self. Critic Anita Myles declares that through the character of Bim, "Anita Desai sends a message to all women – not to be cowed down by the problems of life but to be stoic and develop the qualities of assertion and self-respect" (47).

Despite the prominence of a nationalistic version of motherhood throughout Clear Light of Day, Bim is not the only character that is associated with a mythical representation or a universal symbol of motherhood. Mira-masi, the widowed aunt who arrives in Old Delhi to become the caretaker of the Das children, emerges as another model, albeit more repressed and thus less likely to find an outlet the way that Bim eventually does. Chakravarty posits that both Bim and Mira-masi represent Desai's attempt to "separate the task of mothering from the biological functions of pregnancy and childbirth" (77). This is an important assertion because it again declares that the societal role of motherhood and the ideologies and mythologies that surround it are not contingent on biological motherhood and can indeed be upheld by single women who are still subscribing to the nurturer role. Desai once more evokes the imagery of bees to describe Mira-masi's bondage:

> "*A drudge in her cell, sealed into her chamber. A grey chamber, woven shut. Here she lived, here she crawled, dragging her heavy wings behind her. Crawled from cell to cell, feeding the fat white larvae that lived in the cells and swelled on the nourishment that she brought them. The cells swarmed with them, with their little tight white glistening lives. And she slaved and toiled, her long wings dragging. The air was filled with the angry buzzing of the queen bee.* (89)"

This metaphorical vision reflects her actual lived experience which Desai characterizes as difficult since she "had been a twelve year old when she married and was a virgin when she was widowed – her young student husband, having left to study in England....caught a cold in the rain one winter night, and died," and, afterwards, "She was left stranded with his family and they blamed her bitterly for his death" (108). Unable ever to consummate her marriage, and regarded by her in-laws as useless, Mira Masi is a tragic character throughout the novel. Her response to moving in with the Das family and taking care of her nieces and nephews is positive, and although she probably realizes she is being used for her caretaking abilities, she appears happy to have someone care about her.

The Vedic image of Gotama, the holy cow and a feminine force, is often described as devoted, compassionate, bountiful and protective, and these characteristics are exactly what Mira-masi exudes, especially in regards to the Das children. Mira-masi mostly entertains the Das children, but she realizes that her occupation offers her no power in greater society and makes her reliant on the Das children: now they had an aunt, handed to them like a discarded household appliance they might find of use. They exchanged deep, understanding looks with each other: they had understood their power over her, they had seen she was buying or begging for their tolerance and patronage. They were not beyond, even at that age, feeling the superiority of their position and of extending their gratitude from that elevated position of power. (105)

In the novel, Mira Masi begs the Das parents to buy a cow in order to give fresh milk to the children and to save money; in the end, "the mother capitulated and the cow arrived, led in by the gardener on a rope to be examined and admired like a new bride" (107). Later there is another telling reference to Mira Masi's connection with the cow when the narrator states, "If they [the Das children] choked her, if they sucked her dry of substance, she would give in without any sacrifice of will – it seemed in keeping with nature to do so" (111). Mira Masi's ability to grant sustenance, her willingness to allow the children literally to suck her dry and the argument that this is both natural and keeping with the nature of things shows just how easily the connection between her and the gotama image of the cow is to make. The narrator also declares of her, "She was the tree, she was the soil, she was the earth" (111). Mira-masi definitely has a connection to the natural world, which the holy cow Gotama has as well. In the actual plot of the novel, the cow that the Das family procured for their use ends up falling into the well, where it is stuck since no one can retrieve it. This leads to a slow death by starvation, a horrific event that haunted Mira-masi and the other Das children as well. Later, when Mira-masi is suffering from the last stages of alcoholism, "she seemed obsessed by the idea of the well – the hidden, scummy pool in which the bride-like cow they had once had, had drowned, and to which she seemed drawn," and that haunting image proves to be a foreshadowing of Mira-masi's future, which will include her death from alcohol, the amount so great that she basically drowns in it (99). And like a supernatural figure, and the cow-bride, she, too, haunts the text after her death, just a wisp of her in Bim's peripheral vision.

The image of Mira-masi as Gotama proves how natural her role as widowed virgin is within Indian society. Although she had a difficult life in which nurturing and caretaking became her only options for survival, she, like the cow, is upheld as a positive image within Indian society for her self-sacrificing attributes. She married fairly well but supposedly brought her bad fortune into the arrangement, resulting in her being widowed before she even had the chance to consummate the relationship. It seems almost fated that she would not be a biological mother and she cannot claim motherhood and wifehood in the same sense that her sister can. She is able to assume the ideological role of motherhood, but only the self-sacrificial model, unlike Bim who is able to see opportunities even within her oppressive context.

Tara, Bim's sister and a main character within the novel, emerges in contrast to Bim's character, as a biological mother and submissive wife. Literary scholar Jenni Valjento characterizes Tara as perceiving "marriage as a way of escaping her doubly marginalized position, not only as the most ordinary and timid child in the family but also as the 'other' to Bim's authoritative conception of female identity" (192). Unlike Bim who refuses to marry her entire life and instead looks for fulfillment in other venues, Tara marries Bakul as soon as she is able. Even as a child, Tara has already internalized the role of mother and wife as the only option available to her: "'I am going to be a mother and knit for my babies,' she declares to both Raja and Bim, only gaining uproariously laughter from each of her siblings" (112). She emerges in this novel as a goddess appropriation and Sita character, reliant on her husband, unable to think independently and reticent to make autonomous decisions. She allows Bakul to take her away from her family in order to escape the somewhat complicated situation at her home, and also to help her transition from girl to woman, only made with her introduction into the world of motherhood. Like Sita she remains under her husband's control, and submissive to his wishes, lthough for Tara this means putting on a face of refinement and diplomacy, traveling the world with her husband and children, and living a lavish lifestyle paid for by Bakul's job, not what many would characterize as a difficult life.

Also, Bakul emerges as a character that clearly cares for Tara and the entire Das family, despite his somewhat sarcastic commentary on their lives, and although Tara can be equated with Sita, this does not seem to make her powerless or completely oppressed. Tara does appear to rely on Bakul much more than he relies on her, and in the novel when Tara is faced with difficult tasks, she feels she "wanted only to turn and flee into that neat, sanitary, disinfected land in which she lived with Bakul, with its set of rules and regulations, its neatness and orderliness. And seemliness too – seemliness" (28). Throughout the novel she is shown as dependent on Bakul for both the material items needed for survival but also the emotional stability necessary for her sanity. Near the end of the story when Tara reacts to Bakul and Bim's interactions, she does so with jealousy and fear: "She sensed it with a small prick of jealousy – a minute prick that simply reminded her how very close she was to Bakul, how entirely dependent on him for her own calm and happiness. She felt very vulnerable" (150). Although this episode makes her appear petty, it also shows Tara's position in her relationship with Bakul and alerts her to the dreadful consequences that would follow any separation between her and Bakul. Tara emerges as a mother who is fulfilled by her roles yet still questions her power and autonomy within that relationship. For her, motherhood is empowering in certain ways and also helped her escape from a difficult home situation and, especially at the end of the novel, reifies her purpose in life. As was stated earlier in the paper, Indian motherhood emerges full of possibilities, both positive and negative for various women, and for Tara this complexity remains true.

Fasting, Feasting

Fasting, Feasting is divided into two portions that focus on seemingly very different families, one in India and one in the United States. The first portion follows Uma, a daughter in the Indian family, while the second part follows her brother Arun, who travels to America to get an education and stays with a typical, suburban family in Massachusetts. It is interesting to note the similarities between the two contexts and also significant to see how Arun acts in each specific environment. Uma, the main character, lives in India with her sister, Aruna, her brother, Arun, and her mother and father. She commonly refers to her mother and father as MamaPapa, since she does not seem to be able to separate out any type of autonomous self on the part of Mama or Papa: "MamandPapa. MamaPapa. PapaMama. It was hard to believe that they had ever had separate existences, that they had been separate entities and not MamaPapa in one breath" ("Fasting" 5). Although they are described as one united entity, it is obvious to everyone in the family that it is not a relationship of equal power, and although Mama is able to voice her own opinions at times, Papa is always the final authority. One can see this through the ritual of the finger bowl described early in the novel, in which only Papa is allowed to participate in; "He is the only one in the family who is given a napkin and a finger bowl; they are emblems of his status" (24).

Scholar K. Meera Bai describes the theme of husband-wife alienation in the novels of Anita Desai and comments that for the women involved in Mama's type of relationship, there is "a perpetual quest for meaning and value of life, an attempt to grasp the incomprehensible and the external existential struggle of the individual" (167-8). For Mama, though, there is an option to change her status within the family and gain power, this being through the conception of a male child. Uma was one of the two girls that Mama became pregnant with pretty early in life, and she did not become pregnant again until she was advanced in age. She was worried about having the child due to the risks involved, but for Papa, there was no other alternative since this could be the boy he had always longed for. He claims "they had two daughters, yes quite grownup as anyone could see, but there was no son. Would any man give up the chance of a son?" ("Fasting" 16). She does end up having a baby boy, and this solidifies her unity with her husband: More than ever now, she was Papa's helpmeet, his consort. He had not only made her his wife, he had made her the mother of his son. What honour, what status. Mama's chin was lifted a little higher in the air, she looked around her to make sure everyone saw and noticed. She might have been wearing a medal. (31)

After the birth of her son, Arun, Mama is content with her status within the family, even if it is still subordinate to Papa. She has proven her worth, provided Papa with the ever-wished-for son and completed her duties as a wife. Although Indian society as a whole no longer validates the killing of female children in order to secure male heirs, it is obvious that having a son is still the most desired result. Indian girls can be seen as liabilities for parents, and as one can see in Uma's unfortunate circumstances, sometimes costing the family money with dowries yet not providing any income for their own upkeep.

Literary critic Asha Choubey writes about Mama in her essay "A Feminist Perspective On Anita Desai's Fasting, Feasting" and notes that for some Indian women, "Aeons of dumb, docile existence renders women incapable to act. They are trained to simply show obedience to the orders of their rules. They sulk, they struggle but they are never freed of their meaningless existence as secondary to their masters" ("A Feminist Perspective" 91). Choubey appears to be commenting on what patriarchy can do to women over long periods of time and generations of oppression, and clearly Mama falls within the same category as the women noted in Choubey's essay. She sees that things are unfair for her daughters at times but feels she has no power to act in opposition to Papa. Her obedience renders her incapable of action and unable to change circumstances.

Uma, the daughter of Mama, is another example of a non-mother figure, much like Bim, Ila Das and Mira-masi, who is compelled to take on caretaking and nurturing roles. Critic M. Q. Khan declares that the central meaning of the novel can only be understood through the complicated life of Uma "who becomes the prototype of Sita and Draupadi in their sufferings.... Like the traditional Indian woman, Uma suffers quietly only to prove her great sense of endurance and stoic acceptance" (380). At the beginning of the novel, Uma is characterized as a seemingly normal Indian girl; she goes to school along with her sister Aruna and also helps out at home. Although Uma enjoys school and learning in general, she is not very successful at it and actually ends up failing multiple times. Mama consoles Uma and tells her that she will be happier at home, helping to take care of her new little brother and the rest of the family until she is married. Uma is disappointed since school also afforded her time outside of the home with other girls her age, and Choubey actually sees her entrapment at home and removal from school as "the end of all her dreams, her aspirations and even her individuality. Before the girl could learn to assert herself, she is burdened with the responsibility of taking care of a baby brother" ("Mothers" 388).

At this point in the novel, Uma only has marriage to look forward to as an escape from the responsibilities she has incurred at home, and her family tries desperately to find her a husband. The two attempts the family makes to marry her off fail miserably and actually end up scamming the family and losing them money. Neighbors criticize Mama and Papa for not realizing that they were being lied to, but Mama laments "I was so happy to find someone for my Uma – after all, her cousin Anamika is already married. I didn't like to wait longer" ("Fasting" 83). Up until this point in the novel, Mama and Papa had followed the usual procedure of marrying the older daughter first and then the younger daughter, but "having cost her parents two dowries, without a marriage to show in return, Uma was considered ill-fated by all and no more attempts were made to marry her off" (96).

Since Uma is unable to secure marriage, the family gives up on her, and Mama turns her focus to marrying off Aruna, while Uma is relegated to the position of the permanent caretaker of her parents and little brother, doomed to be at the mercy of her parent's wishes for the rest of her life. Scholar Jyoti Nandan comments on this turn of events for Uma and argues that "daughters in this society are denied autonomy....Daughters are seen as possessions – to be used in a manner which suits the parents. Having failed to get [her] married, Uma's parents use her to make life more comfortable for themselves. The novel hints at the fate of women who remain single in this society" (171). His point does not remain true for every Indian daughter, but for Uma, it does. She is not powerful within this society since she is unmarried, childless, and not smart enough to finish out school and make a career for herself the way Dr. Dutt, the single female doctor in town does. Even when Dr. Dutt gives her the opportunity to work as the warden of a nursing facility that houses girls, her family will not allow her to give up her caretaking duties. Anita Myles argues that "broken, dejected, frustrated, isolated, alienated and lonely Uma stands nowhere, neither falling in the category of unmarried girls, nor in that of married women" (56).

The characters of Uma and Mama are clearly reflected in the American landscape that Arun adventures to in order to fulfill his education obligations. The suburban family he lives with while on summer vacation from the University of Massachusetts, the Pattons, provide a unique comparison to his own family in India. The mother of the family, Mrs. Patton, is clearly linked to Mama by her inability to stand up to her husband and her timid and submissive behavior. Unlike what most people would assume in the case of an American context, as scholar Choubey states.

In a country of supposedly strong and independent women Mrs. Patton has made compromises over every small matter. She is not free even in her choice of food. An ardent vegetarian, she has meekly taken to non-vegetarian food because Mr. Patton feels that that is the only kind of food. All her life Mrs. Patton yearned for vegetarian food but out of fear of disturbing the peace of her home, she did not do anything about it. ("A Feminist Perspective" 94)

Obviously this comparison is being made to Mama, who acquiescently follows the decisions of Papa without question and often forgoes her own wishes and comforts in order to allow for his. Arun notices this similarity as well: "That too, was something Arun knew and had experience of, even if a mirror reflection of it – his father's very expression, walking off, denying any opposition, any challenge to his authority, his stony wait for it to grow disheartened, despair – and disappear" ("Fasting" 186). In another instance, "She [Mrs. Patton] smiles a bright plastic copy of a mother-smile that Arun remembers from another world and another time, the smile that is tight at the corners with pressure, the pressure to perform a role, to make him eat, make him grow, make him worth all the trouble and effort and expense" (194). These two observations made by Arun in reference to Mrs. Patton not only show that he, rejects the male privilege that has been bestowed upon him but also that he realizes that although America and India are completely different contexts with different histories, ideologies and daily realities, motherhood and the pressure to perform a certain role can be equally and comparatively constraining within both contexts.

Melanie Patton, the daughter of the American family, also provides a means of comparison, in her case to the character of Uma. Uma and Melanie are completely different women who have varied priorities, goals and desires, but what does compare is their position within the family and greater society. Asha Choubey compares the two characters and declares; Like Uma this girl [Melanie] also becomes the victim of parental indifference. Her need and thirst for a little love and affection is as intense as that of Uma but unfortunately it is as much in vain as that of her Indian counterpart. On the Indian scene a normal, healthy Uma becomes a patient of Globus Hystericus (Hysteria) and on the Western side the insatiated desire for parental affection and attention, makes Melanie a victim of anorexia and bulimia. ("A Feminist Perspective" 95)

Both characters feel unfulfilled by the social roles they are obligated to fill, undesirable since they do not receive the love and attention they deserve and angry since they do not have the power even to protest against their mistreatment. At the end of the novel, Arun finally realizes that Melanie is truly suffering in her wanderings to find purpose and love in life. He looks at her and notices: A resemblance to the contorted face of an enraged sister who, failing to express her outrage against neglect, against misunderstanding, against inattention to her unique and singular being and its hungers, merely spits and froths in ineffectual protest. How strange to encounter it here, Arun thinks, where so much is given, where there is both license and plenty. ("Fasting" 214)

By providing four characters in this novel that can be grouped into pairs and compared to each other, Desai makes the argument that Indian and American contexts are not actually that different for women, and societal roles for women are equally constraining in both places. Despite the complete difference in circumstances, experiences, ideologies and histories, Uma and Melanie and Mrs. Patton and Mama provide the reader with an investigation of power structures and how certain women under patriarchy allow the actual propagation of patriarchy. Anita Myles states that specifically Uma and Melanie "present two women of different cultures each reacting to the claustrophobic unwanted social norms in their own way. However, both lack sufficient power and hence fail to emerge out successfully in the efforts to rebel against the existing social norms" (58). Through the characters of Mrs. Patton and Melanie, one can gain greater insight into the characters of Mama and Uma, and see that although their situations differ, they are still part of the same mechanisms and ideologies that keep women subservient and acquiescent in their relegation to a submissive role within the family.

In Fasting, Feasting the characters Mira-masi, Aruna and Anamika also provide material for the discussion of Indian motherhood although they are more minor characters than the characters mentioned above. Mira-masi is Uma's widowed aunt, and she comes to visit the family periodically as she conducts pilgrimages. As a widow, there are certain expectations in Indian society, and she willingly fulfills these with a zealous religious devotion to the Hindu god Shiva. The narrator describes her "safe in her widow's white garments, visiting one place of pilgrimage after another like an obsessed tourist of the spirit, and only too often her hapless relatives by marriage found themselves in her way, at convenient stopping places" ("Fasting" 38-9). Mira-masi, not uncommonly, feels almost a lover's connection to Shiva, and it is obvious that for her religion exists as a means of validation, love, affection, communication and power. She even tries to get Uma involved and after a hysterical fit of Uma's, claims that she is Shiva's lover, never to be touched by a human man. Although Mama and Papa discredit this, for Uma it is the only time in her life she is ever desired by a man. Mira-masi also feels that Shiva is the only man for her, so much so that when she loses her beloved idol towards the middle of the novel, she is in despair. Uma describes the scene stating, "Mira-masi let out a sigh so deep it seemed to tear the heart out of her chest. Folding her hands together, she began to pray for the return of her stolen idol, her Lord, her god, in tones of such anguish that Uma crawled away in order not to hear. She was afraid Mira-masi might become hysterical" (138).

Although religion is sometimes referred to as a way to control the masses and keep them complacent, religion is both important and empowering for Mira-masi. Anita Myles agrees and declares that women "turn towards religion for the required succour to sustain not only themselves but also their families. In portraying the religious sensibility in her women characters Anita Desai exhibits her strong inclination towards the Indian way of life in which religion and traditions have their own importance" (54). Although the widowed Mira-masi in Clear Light of Day does not appear to have these same opportunities due to her lack of familial support (especially on her husband's side) and the fact that she was left with nothing after her husband died and was forced to earn her keep within the homes of others, for the Mira-masi in Fasting, Feasting, religion becomes a way to remain independent and autonomous but also contained within a communal group where love and support can be given and received.

Aruna, Uma's sister, lives a life much different from that of her sister and ends up fulfilling all the roles that her sister never could. She marries well, a wealthy man, has children, and appears, at least on the outside, to be a devoted mother and wife. From what Uma perceives, though, marriage is not ultimately fulfilling for Aruna, even though she does everything she is supposed to do. Uma claims that "Aruna had a vision of a perfect world in which all of them – her own family as well as Arvind's – were flaws she was constantly uncovering and correcting in her quest for perfection" (109). Also Uma notices that motherhood "Certainly brought her no pleasure: there was always a crease of discontent between her eyebrows and an agitation that made her eyelids flutter" (109). For Aruna, the only option was education and then marriage and then motherhood, and the family put pressure on her to perform these sanctioned roles, especially since Uma had failed so terribly to complete them. This pressure to be the perfect daughter, wife, and mother appears to have made her into a controlling person who is never satisfied with her life. She is not able to enjoy the fulfillment of her social duty because in the end it proved to be unrewarding for her.

Lastly, Uma's cousin Anamika also provides material for the discussion of motherhood and how dangerous seeking it can actually be for some women. Anamika is described as a wonderful child who is sweet, excels at school, and is thoughtful towards everyone. Anamika actually does so well in school that she is offered a scholarship to Oxford, and although her family would never let her attend, it is used to secure even better marriage prospects for her. In actuality, Anamika's marriage proves to be unfulfilling, abusive, and dangerous. Anamika marries a man who ends up being both verbally and physically abusive, whose mother is also completely disrespectful and cruel as well. Asha Choubey examines Anamika's marriage in her essay "A Feminist Perspective on Anita Desai's Fasting, Feasting" and contends that "Men marry, not because they need a companion or a soul-mate but because marriage gives them a license to show power. Thus politics enters into marriages. Anamika is also an instrument for her husband 'to enhance his superiority to other men'" (97). This obviously does not characterize every marriage in India but remains a problem for many Indian and American women, who suffer at the hands of a malicious husband.

What makes the life of Anamika particularly telling in regards to Indian motherhood specifically is both the role of the mother-in-law in Anamika's life and also what happens to her after she becomes unable to bear children. Anamika's mother-in-law becomes a tyrant in her life and an inescapable force to be reckoned with. Earlier, I discussed the importance of bearing a son for the character Mama; Anamika's mother-in-law has likewise gained power through her conception and birth of a male child. Becoming a mother-in-law not only means retaining power over the son and maintaining high status of oneself in one's husband's eyes, but also gaining power over another woman, the son's wife. In Image of Woman in the Indo-Anglian Novel, Shirwadkar discusses the role of the mother-in-law: As a son's mother an Indian woman enjoys a high position in the family. When the son's wife comes the son is likely to follow the wishes of his wife. The mother is generally unwilling to allow the son to go under her daughter-in-law's power. To that end, she devises various ways to keep him in power or else she harasses the daughter-in-law. (101)

Although the practices that Anamika has to endure on part of this mother-in-law and within the extended family setup are cruel, it is easy to understand why Indian mothers are so unwilling to give up the power they gained when they produced a male child. It is one of the few means available to Indian mothers that can actually increase one's worth in the family and prove one's status as a good, dutiful mother, and many mother-in-laws fight to keep that hard-won status bestowed upon them at the birth of their son. Sadly, this power struggle between Anamika, her husband, and her mother-in-law proves deadly for Anamika. After she finally gets pregnant, Anamika's husband beats her so severely she suffers a miscarriage and in the process becomes barren. The narrator describes the episode by commenting, "she could not bear more children. Now Anamika was flawed, she was damaged goods. She was no longer perfect. Would she be sent back to her family? Everyone waited to hear" ("Fasting" 71).

Once Anamika has no possibility of ever becoming a biological mother, her worth within her marriage is completely devalued. She is seen as an investment not capable of a return. Scholar Elizabeth Jackson also notes that the community's reaction is telling: "they wonder if she will be sent back to her family – not choose to return because she has any say in the matter, but be sent back because she is 'damaged goods', now and unable to bear children" (35). The family and community's embarrassment is relieved, however, by the sudden "suicide" of Anamika, who apparently awoke early one morning to burn herself alive. Neighbors believed that it was actually Anamika's husband and mother-in-law in collusion who committed the murder, but, regardless, her tragic death stands as a testament to the fate that awaits women who are for some reason or another cannot become mothers but are expected to by both their husbands and Indian society.

CONCLUSION

This book sought to explore the realm of Indian motherhood within the fiction of Anita Desai and Indian Literature in English in general, and present the complicated ideologies and histories that inform its position. Anita Myles states "The novelist (Desai) makes it clear that there is no simple, straight forwards solution to the dilemma of woman. It is the awakening of her consciousness which imparts the required strength to conquer the bastion of male dominance" (60). Like Anita Myles, I agree that there is no conclusive way Indian motherhood can be explained or defined, due to its immense complexity. Furthermore, defining Indian motherhood as only an oppressive construct or, in contrast, only an empowering construct, is not helpful for doing nuanced research or for understanding the actual lived reality of Indian mothers. Through the fiction of Anita Desai and specifically the three novels this project focused on, one is able to see how motherhood functions in Indian society, and what informs its construction but also how difficult it is to speak of motherhood in generalities.

Completing the research necessary to this project also reified the belief that there cannot be an overarching category of women or mother. Even in similar contexts or situations there are different histories, ideologies, mythical constructions and actual lived experiences. In order to understand Indian motherhood and have the ability to both critique its failings and celebrate its successes, one cannot merely ascribe characteristics to all Indian women or even all Indian mothers, and must explore the complex, often contradictory realm of Indian motherhood. This type of research is also necessary to avoid homogenization and essentialism, especially for those outside of the context of Indian society. In conclusion, this paper has operated as an exploration of Indian motherhood, which sought to dispel essentialist misrepresentations and truly understand the societal role of mother and it has successfully portrayed the both the intricacy and heterogeneity of the ideological construct of Indian motherhood.

IV
CONCLUSION

This book sought to explore the realm of Indian motherhood within the fiction of Anita Desai and Indian Literature in English in general, and present the complicated ideologies and histories that inform its position. Anita Myles states "The novelist (Desai) makes it clear that there is no simple, straight forwards solution to the dilemma of woman. It is the awakening of her consciousness which imparts the required strength to conquer the bastion of male dominance" (60). Like Anita Myles, I agree that there is no conclusive way Indian motherhood can be explained or defined, due to its immense complexity. Furthermore, defining Indian motherhood as only an oppressive construct or, in contrast, only an empowering construct, is not helpful for doing nuanced research or for understanding the actual lived reality of Indian mothers.

Through the fiction of Anita Desai and specifically the three novels this project focused on, one is able to see how motherhood functions in Indian society, and what informs its construction but also how difficult it is to speak of motherhood in generalities. Completing the research necessary to this project also reified the belief that there cannot be an overarching category of women or mother. Even in similar contexts or situations there are different histories, ideologies, mythical constructions and actual lived experiences. In order to understand Indian motherhood and have the ability to both critique its failings and celebrate its successes, one cannot merely ascribe characteristics to all Indian women or even all Indian mothers, and must explore the complex, often contradictory realm of Indian motherhood.

This type of research is also necessary to avoid homogenization and essentialism, especially for those outside of the context of Indian society. In conclusion, this paper has operated as an exploration of Indian motherhood, which sought to dispel essentialist misrepresentations and truly understand the societal role of mother and it has successfully portrayed the both the intricacy and heterogeneity of the ideological construct of Indian motherhood.

V
WORKS CITED

Acharya, Shata. "Problems of the Self in the Novels of Anita Desai." *Indian Women Novelists.*

Ed. R.K. Dhawan. Vol. 2. New Delhi: Prestige, 1991. (50-67). Print.

Alexander, Meena. "Outcaste Power: Ritual Displacement and Virile Maternity in Indian Women Writers." Economic and Political Weekly. 24.7 (1989): 367-372. Print.

Bai, K. Meera. "Husband Wife Alienation in the Novels of Nayantara Sahgal and Anita Desai."

Indian Women Novelists. Ed. R.K. Dhawan. Vol. 1. New Delhi: Prestige, 1991. (167-76).Print.

Chakravarty, Radha. "Figuring the Maternal: "Freedom" and "Responsibility" in Anita Desai's Novels." *ARIEL.* 29.2 (1998): 75-91. Print.

Chanda, Geetanjali S. "Mapping Motherhood: The Fiction of Anita Desai." *Journal of the Association for Research on Mothering.* 4.2 (2002): 73-83. Print.

Choubey, Asha. "A Feminist Perspective on Anita Desai's *Fasting, Feasting." Critical Responses to Anita Desai.* Ed.

Shubha Tiwari. New Delhi: Atlantic, 2004. (87-98). Print. ---. "Mothers and Daughters: A Comparative Critique of *Fasting, Feasting* and *Difficult*

Daughters." *Critical Responses to Anita Desai.* Ed. Shubha Tiwari. New Delhi: Atlantic, 2004. (383-93). Print.

Desai, Anita. "A Secret Connivance." *The Times Literary Supplement* 14-20 September 1990: 972, 976. Print.

"The Indian Writer's Problems." *Indian Women Novelists.* Ed. R.K. Dhawan. Vol. 2. New Delhi: Prestige, 1991. (7-10). Print.

---*Clear Light of Day.* London: Vintage, 2001. Print.

---*Fasting, Feasting.* New York: Houghton Mifflin, 2000. Print.

---*Fire on the Mountain.* New York: Harper & Row, 1977. Print.

Dhawan, R.K. "Introduction: Indian Women Novelists." *Indian Women Novelists.* Ed. R.K.

Dhawan. Vol. 1. New Delhi: Prestige, 1991. (7-26). Print.

Dutta, Sangeeta. "Relinquishing the Halo: Portrayal of Mother in Indian Writing in English." *Economic and Political Weekly.* 25.43 (1990). Print.

Gupta, Ramesh Kumar. "Trauma of a Housewife: Anita Desai's *Fire on the Mountain.*" *Critical Responses to Anita Desai.* Ed. Shubha Tiwari. New Delhi: Atlantic, 2004. (106-13).Print.

Gupta, Santosh. "Women Writing About Women: Feminist Perspective in Indian Women's Novel in English." *Women about Women in Indian Literature in English.* Ed. Ram S.

Singh and Charu S. Singh. New Delhi: Anmol Publications, 1998. (73-90). Print.

Jackson, Elizabeth. *Feminism and Contemporary Indian Women's Writing.* Basingstoke, [U.K.] Palgrave Macmillan,

2010. Print.

Kanwar, Asha. "Anita Desai and Virginia Woolf: A Comparative Study." *Indian Women Novelists*. Ed. R.K. Dhawan. Vol. 3. New Delhi: Prestige, 1991. (7-21). Print.

Khan, M.Q. "A Critique of *Fasting, Feasting*." *Critical Responses to Anita Desai*. Ed. Shubha Tiwari. New Delhi: Atlantic, 2004. (375-82). Print.

Kumar, Ashok. "Women Empowerment through Indo-Anglican Literature." *Critical Responses to Feminism*. Ed. Binod Mishra. New Delhi: Sarup & Sons, 2006. (19-32). Print.

Kumar, Brajesh. "Feminist Perspectives in the Novels of Anita Desai." *Critical Responses to Feminism*. Ed. Binod Mishra. New Delhi: Sarup & Sons, 2006. (64-72). Print.

Kundu, Rama. "The Ideology of Space in *Fire on the Mountain*." *Critical Responses to Anita Desai*. Ed. Shubha Tiwari. New Delhi: Atlantic, 2004. (147-67). Print.

Liddle, Joanna. "Feminism, Imperialism and Orientalism: the Challenge of the 'Indian Woman'." *Women's History Review* 7.4 (1998): 495-519. Print.

Loomba, Ania. "En-Gendering India: Woman and Nation in Colonial and Postcolonial Narratives." *MLQ*. 63.3 (2002): 396-400. Print.

Narayan, Uma. *Dislocating Cultures: Identities, Traditions, and Third-World Feminism*. New York: Routledge, 1997. Print.

Paul, Premila and R. Padmanabhan Nair. "Varieties of Loneliness in *Fire on the Mountain*."

Indian Women Novelists. Ed. R.K. Dhawan. Vol. 3. New Delhi: Prestige, 1991. (216-35). Print.

Poonacha, Veena. "Rites De Passage of Matrescence and Social Construction of Motherhood: Coorgs in South India." *Economic and Political Weekly*. 32.3 (1997): 101-110. Print.

Sharma, P.P. "From Stereotype to Authentic Selfhood: Changing Images of Women." *Women about Women in*

Indian Literature in English. Ed. Ram S. Singh and Charu S. Singh.
New Delhi: Anmol Publications, 1998. (185-202). Print.

www.ingramcontent.com/pod-product-compliance
Lightning Source LLC
Chambersburg PA
CBHW022059150726
47990CB00003B/1161